Set Yourself Free From Anxiety

Do you constantly feel stressed out?
Does the thought of your daily responsibilities seem terrifying?
Anxiety is not uncommon today and it can be truly unbearable,
but there is a solution.
With this amazing guide you will learn how to take control over
your emotions and thoughts so you can be free of stress and
anxiety, and become the best version of yourself.
The book will provide you with all the essential knowledge to
understand the causes of anxiety, and with the best advice
and strategies to manage your stress and learn how to fight it.
This carefully designed guide will give you the confidence you
need and the strength to remove negativity and to remain
calm even under excessive stress, so you can enjoy your life
and be happy.

Table of contents

Chapter One – What is Anxiety Disorder?

Imagine this – you're strapped into a seat for a roller coaster ride. The car has just begun to move and is making its slow ascent to the top before it crashes down the rail in a topsy-turvy journey of excitement and exhilaration.

Feel the butterflies in the pit of your stomach building with every rail your car rides. As you reach the top, your heart begins to race, and you find that you're short of breath from the thrill you're expecting to begin at any moment.

Now, imagine that you're stuck on that track at the very top. There's a power fault which caused you to stall, and you don't know when the ride is going to continue, and as you wait for the roller-coaster to start again, your heart thuds and your palms become sweaty.

What if you were stuck at the top of that roller coaster for the rest of your life? What if that ride never resumed, and you were doomed to feel those butterflies, that agonising uncertainty and fear of 'what next', all your life.

Think of yourself at the grocery store, waiting in line to pay for your purchases, and feeling that fretfulness and worry in the pit of your stomach. Put yourself in a park, surrounded by little children running around you, and suffering bouts of fear and uneasiness, wondering if you've locked the door after you. Imagine yourself in the shower, and feeling an unreasonable fear that the water from the showerhead is going to drown you.

Now, imagine yourself living this intensified fear, this agonising worry, the uneasiness of feeling something is not right, every single day, and every single moment.

That is what people living with an anxiety disorder suffer from each day.

Generalised Anxiety Disorder is a disorder, a mental ailment – it is not something the sufferer brings upon themselves. The anxiety they feel is not an emotion that can be controlled. It is an endless suffering, of feeling that dread and uneasiness of being at the top of the roller coaster in everyday life.

A patient diagnosed with GAD does not really have a reason to feel anxious. It is a form of diffused anxiety which constantly hovers over the individual for no apparent reason. Unlike normal anxiety which results from an event such as waiting for an important exam result, GAD patients experience the terrible agony and worry without reason.

That is the most difficult stage of GAD, not having a reason for the terrible anxiety, for it means suffering the distress of worry and fear without an end. The simplest of tasks overwhelm the individual – getting up to make breakfast for the family, driving to work, or even sitting down for lunch with office colleagues. The day seems filled with worry and tension beyond their control.

The most common remark people suffering from anxiety disorders get to hear is to stop thinking about it. However, this disorder exists because the thought process cannot be stopped. Regardless of whether the individual is trying to function normally, working on lessening their anxiety, or having a full-blown anxiety attack, the thoughts run through their mind in a non-stop loop.

The most important thing to understand about anxiety is that it is beyond control. Anxiety Disorders are caused by external environmental factors, combined with the emotional well-being of the individual. This could be a simple factor, such as a change of workplace, moving to a different city, or even having a new baby.

Along with external factors, the genetic make-up, personality and the biological chemistry of the brain also matter when treating anxiety disorders. However, this does not mean that a sufferer is emotionally weak, or that they have a medical history of mental illnesses. Anxiety Disorders are triggered by a variety of factors, all coming together at the same time.

Anxiety, by itself, is not an enemy of the body. It acts as a warning signal to the body when danger is near. It prompts the body to prepare you to tune into the fight or flight mode. In a world where instinct and fear form a vital part of life's survival mechanism, anxiety is a very important emotion.

But it is when this emotion spills over in such a way that the worry and tension begin to occur without reason, or become exaggerated for reasons unknown, that it becomes a problem and is diagnosed as an Anxiety Disorder. So how do you differentiate between normal anxiety and an anxiety disorder?

Normal anxiety does not cause you to freeze during your daily activities; facing a cashier or taking a drink of water would not cause you to have irrational fears. The worry and tension that accompanies normal anxiety can be controlled, it is not something that takes over your day-to-day activities, overshadowing all other thoughts.

Normal anxiety also does not lead your worrying to reach extreme lengths that cause unnecessary stress to the body. A delayed reply to an email is just that, a delayed reply to an email. To someone suffering from GAD, a delayed reply would be a catastrophe leading to paranoia and terrible imaginings as to why the reply is delayed.

This is because normal anxiety is usually restricted to realistic scenarios, limited to situations which are probable. They are not diffused and irrational, existing for no reason. When you do feel anxiety, it would last only for a short while and subside when realised. On the other hand, GAD would cause the worry to be never-ending, stretching for months at a time in a continuous cycle of fear and worry, day in and out.

For a layman, trying to understand anxiety is very difficult. It is complicated to imagine not being able to stop feeling anxious. It seems difficult to grasp why someone would feel anxiety if they had no reason to actually be worrying.

So, what is anxiety disorder? To be better able to place yourself in a sufferer's shoes, and be empathetic to the problem they face, try to place yourself in the following scenarios:

- Imagine that you are sitting on a plane, and someone sitting in front of your seat takes something out of a bag in the overhead cabin. A small strap of the bag stays stuck in the door of the overhead cabin, hanging in the air. How would you react?
For a person suffering from anxiety, this could pose a very big issue. They would imagine that the strap would stop the cabin door from locking, and during turbulence, the heavy bags in the cabin could fall out and into someone's head, causing trauma or injury.

- If you have previously suffered from trauma, for instance, a car accident, then you would be able to have compassion for an individual who suffers intense anxiety because they fear the trauma recurring. The fear sets in the mind to such a crippling extent that it hampers their everyday life. A sufferer of PTSD caused by a car accident would feel severe anxiety about travelling in a car. Even getting into a car would be a cause for hyperventilation due to intense anxiety and fear.

PTSD is a form of phobia of the occurred trauma, combined with anxiety about having to do the task which caused the trauma. For a victim of a car accident, this would translate to an intense fear of travelling by cars, and anxiety about having to use cars in their everyday life.

- Imagine suffering from anxiety in your everyday life, but being unable to pinpoint why you're feeling so anxious. It is an uneasiness you feel in the pit of your stomach, a gnawing fear which makes your hands tremble, but there is nothing in your life that can cause you to worry in this manner.

Oftentimes, the anxiety faced by persons suffering from GAD is without reason. This is a form of diffused anxiety which continues to hover in a person's mind expressly because there is no reason for it to exist. It is an unwarranted fear in the individual's mind.

These are but a few examples of the problems people suffering from Anxiety Disorder face. The important thing to know is that this is a disorder that can be treated, both by modern medicine as well as techniques that can be applied at home.

However, before we discuss how Anxiety Disorders can be treated, it is important to understand a different kind of anxieties that exist and to identify which type of anxiety the individual is suffering from.

In the next chapter, we will study the different forms of anxiety that exist.

Chapter Two – Anxiety Disorders and Its Forms

As we have seen, it is normal for a person to feel anxiety from time to time. In fact, a little bit of anxiety is good for you. It prompts you to stay active, take action and resolve problems. However, when it begins to hamper an individual's daily life by being unreasonable or crashing in on them without reason, it is the time that they seek help.

There are six types of Anxiety Disorders, each with their own distinct symptoms. Dividing this into different forms which make it easier to diagnose a patient. Do any of the below scenarios sound familiar?

- Lina wakes up early in the morning because she feels a dread and uneasiness while in bed. She cannot bear to stay lying down, as the worry and tension are causing her restlessness. There is no reason for her to be feeling so worried and anxious. Her children are safe at home and in their beds. Her husband is loving and doing well at his work. Everything in her life is smooth, and yet, the anxiety persists.

Feeling such a constant gnaw of anxiety, an unsettled feeling in the pit of your stomach, or an unrelenting uneasiness keeping you on edge is a symptom of Generalised Anxiety Disorder. Lina would most probably also be suffering from pain in her neck, shoulders and upper back, caused by constant tension in those muscles, and a feeling of breathlessness, which is a physical manifestation of the severe anxiety she is suffering.

GAD is the most common form of Anxiety Disorders found amongst individuals.

- Alex wants to go to the club with his friends over the weekend, but an intense fear of facing strangers holds him back. What if the people he meets not like him, or what if he is not able to make intelligent conversation? And how will he order even a drink at the bar from the bartender, when he can't make eye contact with his own friends?

If you find that you are hit by bouts of shyness so intense, that it disrupts your everyday life, to the point that you fear walking out of your house, or avoid eye contact with people to feel safe, you might be suffering from Social Anxiety. Like Alex, the anxiety in facing people or having any social contact is caused by the fear of being judged, looked at or commented upon, to the point of being obsessed by these thoughts and the negativity surrounding them even when you're not present in a social situation.

Social Anxiety is not defined by your emotions. It is a behavioural pattern. For instance, consider the following scenarios:

- Not having a liking to going out too often

- Not having too many friends

- Preferring to stay at home over a weekend rather than go on a holiday

- Not making new friends easily

These are scenarios where a person is healthy and does not have Social Anxiety. A person could be an introvert but not having Social Anxiety. A person could also be shy, but not to the extent that they have difficulty in going about their day to day lives. Compare this to the following:

Not being able to talk to people, including your friends
Wanting to go out, but having a phobia of meeting people
Worrying about what others think of you constantly, to the point you avoid company
Having difficulty in making and maintaining eye contact with people

These situations are different because the individual is suffering because of their anxiety. These chronic anxiety symptoms, though irrational, and recognised by the individual to be irrational, refuse to go away, causing the individual to have Social Anxiety.

- Mona is at the pharmacy, waiting in line to pay for her purchases. The air is calm, and a soft music is playing on the overhead speakers. As she stands in the queue, Mona is hit by a sudden breathlessness, and her hands begin to shake. She has to step out of line to stand against the wall, because she finds that she is suddenly dizzy, and feeling sick. A strange sensation of the world freezing takes over her, and sweat begins to run down her back as a tightness in her chest begins to turn into pain.

A disorder often confused with GAD but quite different from it, is the Panic Disorder. This is a disorder that is characterised by short periods of severe panic, causing both physical and mental turmoil that can, in extreme cases, even lead to hospitalisation. Once again, this is neither a thought that can be controlled nor is it caused by real situations.

Like Mona, persons suffering from this disorder often find themselves victims of frequent panic attacks not caused by any real reason. The symptoms are elevated heart rate, a sensation of floating outside your body, light-headedness, and freezing during the attack. The hardest part of suffering from this disorder besides suffering from panic attacks is fearing the arrival of the next attack.

A panic attack is characterised by a sudden onslaught of fear accompanied by breathlessness and chest pain. The symptoms mimic those of a heart attack and can give anxiety regarding their health to the sufferer. Like anxiety, panic by itself is not a bad emotion.

Panic is the trigger for that unusual mode which is often experienced in situations of extreme danger. It is when these attacks start to occur without reason on a regular basis, that it becomes a problem.

- Demi is sitting at home reading a book. It is a sunny day outside, and she wants to go for a walk in the garden. However, simply the thought of stepping out of the confines of the four walls of her home bring on severe anxiety, and cause her to feel breathless and stressed out.

This form of anxiety disorder is Agoraphobia, which is an intense fear of being outside your own home. A debilitating fear of stepping out of the confines of your home for mundane tasks such as a walk in the garden, collecting a delivery, or going to the grocery store signals that the individual may be suffering from Agoraphobia.

Agoraphobia is closely related to claustrophobia, despite being the exact opposite of it. Claustrophobia is the fear of closed spaces, such as tunnels and changing rooms. Agoraphobia is the fear of open spaces. Yet, persons suffering from Agoraphobia also find that they cannot tolerate crowds which press closely to them.

They also have difficulty in adjusting to closed spaces outside their own homes, such as shopping centres and movie theatres.

An advanced form of Agoraphobia can also lead to Panic Disorders, as facing a place outside their homes causes the sufferer to have panic attacks. This, in turn, leads them to avoid the place where they had the panic attack to prevent the attack from recurring.

Do not confuse Agoraphobia with Social Anxiety. Social Anxiety is anxiety caused by being out in public for fear of being judged. Agoraphobia is anxiety caused by having to step outside the home.

- Sara touches the doorknob on her way out of the house. Touching the doorknob is a ritual she is bound by; not touching it could result in her mum's health worsening. She takes measured breaths on her way to the bus stop. Breathing in while looking at a bee flying above a flower, and breathing out while looking away from it will cause her to be very anxious and uneasy.

An anxiety which is linked to an obsession or compulsion is a sign of Obsessive Compulsive Disorder. The individual suffering from this finds themselves a victim of a thought pattern, whereby an anxiety provoking thought is shaken away by a certain ritual, such as touching a favourite pen, or walking in a particular way when stepping out of the house. Any break in the ritual causes overwhelming anxiety, and uneasiness, binding the patient in a prison of the ritual.

Unfortunately, what begins as a way to ward off anxiety becomes a repetitive behaviour which cannot be broken. The ritual only provides temporary relief to the mind before returning with an overwhelming rush of anxiety.

It has been suggested that a method to control the OCD is by breaking the ritual, one step at a time. This would cause mental distress and anxiety, which is the brain healing itself. For instance, an individual who has an OCD to wash their hands every few minutes should not do so the next time the urge arises.

This would cause anxiety and uneasiness, but by not reinforcing the behaviour, the brain would rewire itself and stop the compulsion as it does with most habits. However, like all other disorders, it is advised to also seek external help to recover from this disorder.

- Bobby had a miscarriage last year. She finds herself unable to talk about it, because the thought of reliving the miscarriage makes her feel breathless, and brings on a panic attack. She also cannot bear to look at small children and avoid all events where she might encounter babies. Her husband wants to try for a baby again, but she is hesitant because she is afraid of having another miscarriage.

A commonly acknowledged form of anxiety is the Post Trauma Stress Disorder or PTSD. The main problem caused by PTSD is emotional trauma, wherein the sufferer becomes emotionally unavailable, as they close themselves to all external emotions in an attempt to protect their mind from the trauma they have suffered. The individual may also experience anxiety over the trauma, and a fear that it may recur, causing them to detach further from their surroundings.

You could describe PTSD as a form of Panic Disorder, where the panic attacks do not stop. It manifests in different forms, such as nightmares, withdrawal from situations which remind of the trauma and flashbacks of the trauma itself.

This is a common disorder in soldiers returning from war, victims of terror attacks and or witnesses, or victims of violent assault. Getting help to the sufferer is of utmost importance, as left untreated, this disorder can turn into a form of severe depression.

While understanding the different types of anxieties is certainly helpful, it is also important to seek help when your symptoms seem beyond your control. Without help, overcoming the symptoms and resuming a normal life is difficult to achieve. As it is said, if you cannot help yourself, you need to seek help from outside.

When we talk about anxiety as an issue, the most common misunderstanding that confuses people is the difference between anxiety, as a Generalised Anxiety Disorder, and Panic Disorder. In the next chapter, we will discuss how you can distinguish between the two, so as to understand how best to differentiate their symptoms.

Chapter Three – Panic Disorder V/S GAD

What is a Panic Disorder?

Panic attacks are common in everyday life. Hitting the send button and recognising that you've sent it to your boss instead of your best friend can cause you to panic. Rumours of a terror attack in a city where your sibling may reside will cause you to panic. A small child at a fun fair will panic if she cannot find her parents.

These are normal circumstances which cause your body to hit the panic button. However, what happens if you're sitting at the park enjoying the breeze, and feel a sudden panic attack hit you out of nowhere, for no apparent reason? A racing heartbeat, sweaty palms, light-headedness, and even chest pain. This would last for a very short time, perhaps only minutes, but it would be enough to disrupt the rest of your day.

And what follows is anxiety. Why did that panic attack happen? What caused it to happen? Will it happen again? When will it happen again?

That is exactly what individuals suffering from Panic Disorder go through in their everyday life. They experience random panic attacks brought on by an over-sensitivity to the sensations they experience in their body or by stress. Oftentimes, the attacks are not even triggered by any external factor. They just occur.

At the same time, the individual also fears an onset of an attack. Not knowing what causes the panic attack to strike, there is no way to predict when it can happen again. This instils such an intense fear in the mind of the sufferer that they find themselves unable to function beyond the tension, worry and fear of expecting the next panic attack.

This leads to either Agoraphobia, wherein the individual fears stepping out of the house in case a panic attack were to strike when they're not ready for it, or a severe anxiety in expectation of the next panic attack.

Characteristically, the Panic Disorder is made up of these two symptoms; experiencing random panic attacks, and fear of the panic attacks.

At the same time, we also have Generalised Anxiety Disorder, that is, anxiety caused by no particular reason. This is an aggravated form of fear and worry for which there is no basis. GAD also functions in the same way, by hitting the sufferer with anxiety attacks, where the individual suffers from bouts of severe anxiety during different periods of the day, not brought on by any external factor.

Some of the symptoms you would feel during an anxiety attack may be similar to those of a panic attack. Elevated heart rate, light-headedness and hopelessness are common for both anxiety and panic.

In anxiety attacks, however, the sufferer would experience an agonising uneasiness, like butterflies in their stomach which would keep them on a constant edge. It is akin to the fear you feel while awaiting an important exam result. You find out your grade, and the anxiety goes away.

In GAD, however, it just the fear multiplied manifold that the individual feels, and as it is diffused anxiety without reason, it continues to gnaw unabated.

To have a better understanding of how Panic Disorder and GAD are different, let us look below at two detailed examples of individuals suffering from these disorders.

Otto finds himself suffering from panic attacks during random moments, for no reason that he can figure out. The last time this had happened was two weeks ago, and he has experienced constant anxiety since then, as he has awaited the next attack. He is now sitting at his home reading a book when he finds himself suddenly short of breath and feeling an adrenaline rush. His heart is thudding hard in his chest, and he is filled with dread and fear. His palms become sweaty, and he begins to feel a tightening in his chest, scaring him that he is about to die of a heart problem.

When he tries to get up and walk to relieve the panic he feels, he finds himself feeling lightheaded and dizzy, and thus unable to stand without support. Instead, he grips at the arms of his chair tightly, waiting for the panic to pass. Within minutes, the overwhelming panic begins to subside, and Otto is able to breathe normally again. However, he has now faced with the anxiety again, knowing, and fearing, that this episode will repeat itself. He also filled with hopelessness at his condition.

The anxiety that Otto feels post his panic attack in the above episode is a form of GAD but differentiated by the fact that his anxiety has a reason. He feels the anxiety because he worries and fears the next panic attack. Unlike GAD which is a diffused form of anxiety, the worry and fear Otto feels are substantiated by a base reason.

Paula is in bed early in the morning when she feels a bud of fear starting to throb in her stomach. Within minutes, the fear has bloomed into a sense of dread and she finds herself unable to keep lying down. A stifling threatens to choke her, and she feels a need to escape the restlessness and uneasiness that seem to have taken residence within her.

The anxiety persists through the day and fills Paula with a sense of hopelessness as she struggles to breathe past the crippling fear and tension gnawing at her. Her heart is racing, and she feels sick and suffers from a loss of appetite. She struggles to complete her daily tasks but is ridden by a constant fear and tension which refuses to go away, reducing her to tears. By the end of the day, the anxiety begins to subside, and she feels almost normal. However, she knows that come tomorrow morning, the restlessness and uneasiness along with the anxiety will be back.

Here, Paula is suffering from GAD. She feels a constant anxiety throughout her day which refuses to go away because there is no reason why she is feeling the way she is. If there were a reason, once the reason was achieved, she would feel better. Right now, however, she is suffering on a daily basis.

As you must have noted in the two examples, there is a distinct difference between Generalised Anxiety Disorder and Panic Disorder.

The first main difference here is that Panic Attacks brought on by the Panic Disorder last for short durations, and are spaced through a few weeks. Anxiety Attacks, on the other hand, last for almost the whole day and recur on a daily basis.

The attacks in themselves are also different.

Panic attacks are sudden, and accompanied by light-headedness, trembling of hands or legs, chest pain, elevated heart rate, sweating, a surreal or out of body sensation, breathlessness, dread and a sense of doom.

Anxiety attacks are slower, last longer, and are accompanied by breathlessness, overwhelming fear, restlessness, uneasiness, nausea, and butterflies in the stomach, trembling extremities and a sense of hopelessness.

Another main difference is that a person suffering from Panic Disorder feels anxiety related to a reason – the fear of the next panic attack. The anxiety takes over their lives, and causes them much trouble, affecting the quality of their life.

On the other hand, persons suffering from GAD do not have a reason for the anxiety that they are suffering of. It makes this disorder that much harder to treat, because there is no basal cause which can be treated, that is, no base reason which can be done away with. The treatment has to wholly focus on lifestyle and behavioural change.

It is also possible that a person suffering from GAD suffers from intermittent panic attacks, as a side effect of the intense anxiety they endure. However, this condition would still be diagnosed with Generalised Anxiety Disorder.

Just as the symptoms as discussed above vary for both the disorders, their causes are also different. In both cases, it is not yet understood what triggers the disorder. It has been studied that genetic make-up of a person, combined with external environmental factors can make a person susceptible to both conditions.

However, the main cause behind the Panic Disorder is the 'Fight or Flight' response of the body. This is what differentiates both conditions, and makes the symptoms also varied. The 'Fight or Flight' response is limited to a short time period by the biology of the brain, that is, the response wanes when the danger passes, or the surge of adrenaline lowers.

Thus, even though a person suffering from Panic Disorder is not in any danger, the panic attack wanes after a short time.

As Anxiety is a response to a fear or worries about circumstances in the daily life of a person, the anxiety attacks that a normal person may have are not limited to any duration. They wane as per the individual's biological chemistry, brain chemistry and environmental factors. Thus, a person suffering from GAD would also suffer from anxiety indefinitely and have constant anxiety attacks as per their daily schedule.

Panic Disorder is classified under Anxiety Disorder only because one of the effects of suffering from the condition is the anxiety the individual feels in between attacks. Thus, you can understand how different the two are.

As the basics of both conditions are different, the treatment for both is very different too. Persons suffering from symptoms of panic are also advised to seek the help from a doctor to rule out their panic symptoms masking major health issues such as:

- Mitral valve prolapse – this is a medical condition related to cardiac arrest and is caused by one of the heart's valves not closing correctly
- Hyperthyroidism (overactive thyroid gland)
- Hypoglycaemia (low blood sugar)
- Stimulant use (amphetamines, cocaine, caffeine)
- Withdrawal from long-term medication

As a treatment option, the following is recommended for persons suffering from Panic Disorders:

- Psychotherapy as a treatment, by regular visits to the psychotherapist

- Use of modern medicine, that is, Selective Serotonin Reuptake Inhibitors (SSRI)
- The treatment can be enhanced with the use of both psychotherapy and SSRI
- Anti-anxiety medication for extreme cases of Panic Disorder
- A Combination of all three options

Let us read on to understand how to counter GAD in the next chapter.

Chapter Four – Tackling Anxiety

For an individual dealing with anxiety on a daily basis, it is difficult to define the agony they suffer. Extreme GAD often precludes depression and a sense of hopelessness of having to live with the worry and tension each day.

Let us go through a comprehensive list of symptoms of persons suffering from GAD:

Excessive anxiety, without a base reason for the worry

Overwhelming fear and uneasiness

Restlessness, and feeling constantly on edge

Tension in upper body muscles leading to pain in neck, shoulders and back from constant stiffness

Headaches and nausea

Loss of appetite

Breathlessness

Irritability

Trembling of extremities, such as fingers or lips

Insomnia or trouble staying asleep

Exhaustion from constantly being restless

Whilst it is known that GAD is diffused anxiety, that is anxiety without reason, there are also triggers which spur an anxiety attack. More often than not, the anxiety once triggered, lingers in a diffused state. For instance, a patient who is staying away from home may that they would never see their sister again.

Once triggered, the anxiety would linger on, and each time the individual thinks of her sister and the distance between them, the anxiety would strengthen, causing the anxiety attack to either recur or worsen.

At the same time, the anxiety would exist in a diffused state, such that the person continues to feel anxious despite not having thoughts of their sister throughout the day. This is because the thought of the patient's sister is only the trigger. It is not the main concern for the person.

Excessive anxiety can also lead to panic attacks, but as we have seen earlier, this does not mean that the individual is suffering from Panic Disorder. The panic attacks are a result of the anxiety going beyond what the individual can handle.

This is important to understand for any treatment to be effective. Anxiety Disorders are treated in mostly the same way that Panic Disorders are treated. The patient is offered the following:

- Psychotherapy as a treatment, by regular visits to the psychotherapist
- Use of modern medicine, that is, Benzos (anti-anxiety medication)
- The treatment can be enhanced with the use of both psychotherapy and Benzos
- If the patient has an advanced case of anxiety and is also suffering from depression, antidepressants may also be prescribed.

Selective Serotonin Reuptake Inhibitors (SSRIs), are a form of anti-depressants which are used to treat depression, unexplained panic attacks and anxiety. For persons suffering from chronic anxiety disorders such as GAD, citalopram

(Celexa), escitalopram (Lexapro), and sertraline (Zoloft) are often prescribed.

SNRIs (serotonin and norepinephrine reuptake inhibitors) are compounds which work to either produce or suppress enzymes in the brain such as serotonin and norepinephrine. Antihistamines and beta-blockers are used in alternate cases where a person's GAD is not severe.

The condition that follows SSRIs or SNRIs is that the tablet has to be taken on a daily basis as long as it has been prescribed by the doctor, regardless of whether the individual is suffering from anxiety attacks on a particular day.

On the other hand, Antihistamines or beta-blockers are prescribed on a per need basis and are to be taken only if the patient is suffering from anxiety, or has identified a trigger for anxiety.

A drug that is prescribed to all patients with chronic anxiety is a set of drugs classified as benzodiazepines; alprazolam (Xanax) and diazepam (Valium). However, taking Benzodiazepines on a regular basis causes side effects such as memory problems, excessive drowsiness and irritability. Taking them in a large dose for a short period of time to overcome severe anxiety is, however, safe.

Whilst it is important to consult a doctor, it is also necessary that the individual tries to overcome anxiety on a personal level. We have here some techniques that are useful for fighting extreme anxiety.

Psychotherapy:

Psychotherapy, as a standalone option or in conjunction with medication, is thought to be a fundamental option of treatment for generalised anxiety disorder. The main point of psychotherapy is to 'talk your way out of anxiety'. Different Talk Therapies have different guide ways.

Out of the multiple therapies that are applied, there are several methods which have been found to be more applicable and effective than others. Psychodynamic psychotherapy and Supportive-expressive therapy are two particular therapies which allow the individual to look at anxiety differently. They prescribe to the worry being an outgrowth of fears and worries about relationships important to the person.

Here we discuss some forms of psychotherapy which are used to effectively treat GAD:

- Acceptance & Commitment Therapy – ACT is a form of 'third-wave' therapy. This is a three part therapy, which focuses on behavioural conditioning and processing in the first two waves, and follows a route of acceptance in the third wave.

ACT is, as the name suggests, an acceptance therapy, in which through talking, the sufferer is guided to accept their disorder. This follows on the theory that when you stop fighting the symptoms, you stop the constant train of thoughts running in your mind about the symptoms. This, in turn, allows for greater psychological flexibility.

Acceptance of your circumstance is designed to protect the mind from anxiety triggers and painful thoughts. As a result, the individual has turned into the patterns of their thoughts, avoidance mechanism, and actions they take. Identifying these patterns allows the sufferer to understand how and what would trigger their anxiety, and how to tackle it more efficiently.

For instance, let us look at Sue who is having triggers which cause anxiety attacks to begin. Thoughts of her mother bring on anxiety, which lasts through the day. By getting Sue to talk about her innermost fears, the psychotherapist would understand what is going on in her mind which causes her to be anxious about her mother.

By identifying what causes her mother to give her anxiety, the psychotherapist would be in a better position to lead Sue's thoughts to think positively.

It is important that to avail ACT, you need to approach a psychologist trained in this type of psychotherapy. Your psychotherapist should be empathetic and be willing to listen and hear you out. At the same, he should be non-judgemental as he guides you through your conversations exploring your anxiety, bringing about an awareness of your emotions.

In a typical session, you will practice mindfulness to look at your thoughts. This means not judging your own thoughts, instead of having a positive awareness of your emotions, memories and sensations. Once your deepest thoughts and fears are identified, the therapist would sit through cognitive exercises to redefine and put into perspective your story, to help you to accept it as what it is – just an experience of life.

- Psychodynamic Psychotherapy: Psychodynamic is based on a theory that the subconscious mind has feelings and thoughts of its own, which can lead to inner conflicts that emerge as anxiety attacks.

This would mean that Sue has worries which she is not consciously aware of, but that are present at the back of her mind, which causes her anxiety. As she is not able to pinpoint at these thoughts because they are not present in her conscious thoughts, the anxiety she feels exists in a diffused form.

By talking about her feelings, and identifying what it is that is present in her sub-conscious mind that causes her to feel anxiety about her mother, Sue would get relief from her anxiety symptoms.

During therapy, a patient is encouraged to talk freely about their feelings and emotions in an attempt to make them aware of their sub-conscious minds. This is an unstructured therapy, and not defined by a carefully crafted script, and may continue over a long period of time.

Individuals availing this therapy find it very effective in reducing anxiety symptoms. However, as the therapy takes a long time to work, and is unstructured, short-term psychodynamic therapy is emerging as a new branch.

- Interpersonal Psychotherapy: IPT was originally designed to treat depression. However, as it was found to be very effective in treating anxiety symptoms arising due to depression, it has been extended for anxiety treatment too.

IPT is a form of therapy which looks at anxiety being a manifestation of the worries and tensions which arise due to problems in relationships. This therapy believes that resolving relationship problems will resolve anxiety issues.

IPT looks at Sue's relationship with her mother as a cause of the anxiety attacks she suffers. By talking about her problems, and improving her relationship, her anxiety would also go away. By understanding the issues in her relationship, Sue's therapist would be able to pinpoint the areas which are causing the anxiety to arise, and how to deal with it.

A typical therapy session can be a personal session with the therapist, or a group therapy session where listening to other sufferers talk about their problems will help the individual identify their own issues.
These are short, concise sessions which are time-limited and focused only on the present life of the person. The patient would ideally talk about a few relationships that are particular to them, and the issues they face in those relationships. The therapy also focuses on improving communication techniques of the patient to improve the overall interpersonal effectiveness in their daily lives.

As such, for persons diagnosed with depression made severe by GAD, IPT is a very effective form of therapy that can be applied.

- Cognitive Behavioural Therapy: CBT is unlike other therapy options, in the sense it focuses on the present and conscious mind of the individual, rather than the sub-conscious. It is a form of structured problem-solving therapy.

Ideally, CBT is a short-term therapy that can be extended to a longer period if the GAD symptoms of the individual wax and wane over a long period of time. The focus of CBT is to enable the sufferer to identify their own problems, in an attempt to make them their own therapist.

This would mean that Sue is suffering from anxiety attacks related to thoughts of her mother because she has active thoughts about her mother – either related to her health, her relationship, or other causes.

By understanding what it on her mind and not avoiding those thoughts, Sue would be able to fight the anxiety symptoms more effectively.

CBT has to be taken from a therapist who is trained in it. Interesting, a therapist can be a psychiatrist, a psychologist or a mental health counsellor. A typical session would be very active, taking the patient on a journey of reflecting upon their issues through educative conversations.

CBT will guide the individual to understand their anxiety better by analysing their own selves, learning to let go and relax, and reining in their thoughts. This is done by using a variety of CBT approaches, learning to stop avoiding facing their fears, and starting to focus on a problem-solving lifestyle for the issues that may cause anxiety.

During the CBT session, the therapist will team up with the individual to agree upon the agenda for the sessions. All sessions will focus on homework, to have the patient practice the techniques that have been studied during the session. The therapist will review the homework to ensure the individual is making an effort too.

The sessions are usually carried out weekly unless the anxiety symptoms are out of control. In such cases, the sessions will be increased to support the sufferer, until the anxiety comes under control. Post the sessions, once the individual recovers from their anxiety symptoms, patients may return to visit with their therapist for 'booster' sessions, as a check-in on their self-therapy.

By talking with their doctor, individuals may identify which form of psychotherapy would be most suitable for them. Alternately, you may understand each type of psychotherapy and decide which one you would prefer referring to help alleviate your anxiety symptoms.

To understand some basic home exercises which persons suffering from GAD may practice, let us go on to the next chapter.

Chapter Five – Dealing with Anxiety with Activity

While anxiety can be dealt with using psychotherapy and modern medicine, it is very important for the individual to also tackle the anxiety symptoms from home. Unless the sufferer makes an attempt to heal themselves, the anxiety will keep returning and make the individual dependent on medicines and therapy.

It is understandable that anxiety causes severe phobia of irrational bases, such as fear of closed spaces, fear of darkness, fear of closing your eyes etc. However, it is important to overcome each fear and face head on to heal yourself from the anxiety attacks.

Home exercises, while being effective in the long run, cannot provide complete relief from anxiety symptoms if the GAD is severe. In cases where the GAD is mild, but the home exercises do not seem to be giving any relief, it is recommended that the individual consults with a doctor lest the symptoms worsen.

Home exercises do provide relief and long-term freedom from anxiety and GAD in conjunction with psychotherapy and modern medicine.

If an individual is suffering from anxiety, they may try some of the exercises given here below:

- Yoga: There cannot be enough stress placed on the effect of yoga to calm the mind. But first, let us understand what yoga is.

Yoga is defined as a spiritual practice to control the breathing technique whilst adopting body postures designed for health & relaxation. What this translates to is that practising yoga helps the individual to practice controlling their breath, which is a very difficult process in anxiety.

As we have read here, one of the symptoms of anxiety is breathlessness. This is a physical manifestation of the mental turmoil, and can in turn itself lead to more anxiety due to fear of not being able to breathe. When this happens, it is important to be able to control your breathing to take deep breaths without feeling suffocated.

At the same time, anxiety also causes intense tension in the shoulders, neck and back. Practising yoga in the different postures called *asana* allows for the release of the tension in those muscles, in turn helping in relaxing of the body and promoting better health.

The reason yoga also works is that it teaches the person in *asana* to focus on the present and to practice mindfulness. Anxiety causes havoc thought processes which lead to further problems such as insomnia and uneasiness. Meditation teaches individuals skills for staying in the moment by counteracting on the tendency to let the thoughts be led astray.

Meditation counteracts anxiety and its symptoms because it is a practice in which the focus is on freeing the mind. It is to concentrate on a *mantra*, or chant, and to stop any other thought from entering the mind.

You can begin by trying out a few simple *asana* at your home. It is best to refer to a yoga instructor or to speak to your doctor before you begin to avoid injuries. These *asana*, however, are basic and would not cause any harm.

- *Dhanurasana* (Bow Pose): For this *asana*, lie on your stomach, flat on the ground. Reach behind your body for your ankles, as you bend your legs on your knees to raise them up. Hold on to your ankles with your hands. Lift your head, and hold steady for a count of 10 seconds. Breathe out as you let go of your legs.

- *Janu Shirshasana* (One-legged forward bend): Stand with your legs apart and face to either side of your body. Bend to the side with your hands straight out to your sides, and touch the toes of your foot with one hand. Hold steady for 10 seconds. Repeat on the other side of your body. This is one set.

- *Balasana* (Child's Pose): Sit on the ground with your knees bent, and your leg folded under your body. Stretch forward, reaching for the floor before you, making sure your hands are straight and stretched as far from your body as possible. Touch the floor with your head and hold steady for 10 seconds.

- *Veerbhadrasana* (Warrior Pose): Stand with your feet apart and turn your whole upper body to one side. Raise both your hands before you without bending them and bend your body down. While you do this, lift the leg on the other side of your body straight up. Stretch your leg behind, as you stretch your hands in front, and hold steady for 10 seconds. Repeat on the other side. This is one set.

- *Shavasana* (Corpse Pose): Lie flat on the ground on your back and breathe deeply. Let your body relax.

Learning to breathe right is as important as practising asana in the correct way. The method of breathing is termed *pranayama*. To practice *pranayama*, sit cross-legged on a flat surface and breathe deeply to drive away stray thoughts from your mind before your begin. Try the breathing techniques given here for relieving anxiety:

- *Kapal Bhati* (Skull Shining breathing): Take, in short, shallow breaths, and blow forcefully out, expelling all the air out of your lungs. Imagine negativity piled in your body and mind being pushed out of your system with the forceful exhalations. The exhalations would also release built up energy generated by anxiety in the pit of your stomach.
- *Nadi Shodhan* (Alternate nostril breathing): With the ring and middle fingers of your right hand joined together, pinch your left nostril shut and breathe in through your right nostril. Release the left nostril as you pinch your right nostril shut with your thumb. Now breathe in with your right nostril and out with your left. This is one set. Repeat as many sets as make you comfortable.
- *Bhastrika* (Fire Breath): Breath in and out deeply for about two and a half seconds each. As you breathe in, imagine soaking in positive energy from your surroundings. As you breathe out, imagine that the toxins piled in your body are being expelled.

It is easy to recommend yoga and to resolve to practice it. However, in the midst of an anxiety attack, actually getting down to calm yourself and place your body in the spiritual positions is not only overwhelming but also fearful.

That is why it is important to practice yoga on a daily basis, regardless of whether the individual is suffering from anxiety on a particular day or not.

- Allot time to your worry: This may sound like a silly suggestion. However, to someone suffering from anxiety because they are not able to stop their thought process, it would be an asset.

As we have read, it is not possible to stop the mind from thinking; it is difficult or impossible to stop the thought processes. At such a time, if an individual trains their minds to assign a worry-time to the irrational thoughts, it would make the anxiety lessen.

Imagine applying worry-time as we have shown below:

- You are working on your garden, and are not able to stop worrying about your son who was bullied at school the previous year. The fear that it could start again this year is making you feel paranoid and bringing on anxiety attacks.

- Your son is not at home right now and you are not able to stop your mind from worrying about what he might be going through at school right now. You are getting defused anxiety every time you think about your son or about his school.

- You stop and tell yourself that you have to work on the garden right now and do not have time to worry about bullying when it has not happened the last six months. You will worry about your son's bullying at 5 pm today for an hour.

- Every time your thoughts turn to your son or to his bullying, you tell yourself that you will think about it at 5 pm and train your mind to refuse to worry.

- At 5 pm, you let yourself feel all the anxiety you have been feeling the whole day, and draw up worry-scripts. At 6 pm your alarm rings and you stop thinking about your son again.

- When you feel your thoughts getting out of hand, you tell yourself you will continue to worry tomorrow at 5 pm.

This practice is difficult to master at the beginning. However, regular practice helps the individual to overcome your thoughts and rein them in.
- Worry Scripts: The worry scripts are a form of transferring your fear and thoughts onto paper.
It has been clinically proven that writing out thoughts helps to get them out of an individual's mind. Similarly, writing out thoughts over which one may have no control would also help to stop them hovering in the mind if they are noted down on paper.
A worry script is a form of a journal, where each day, the individual would write out in great detail their worries and fears, which are both irrational and difficult to stop thinking about.
Persons suffering from GAD try to push their difficult to control thoughts out of their mind, which costs a lot of energy and is futile. The thought would return as soon as the effort to push the thought away starts to wane. Alternately, the individual would attempt to change their thought process by changing the thought they have in their mind. However, as happens in GAD, the only thoughts in their minds are worries and fears. As such, changing the thought process would not work.
A worry script is different precisely because it does not attempt to banish the thought in any manner. It puts the fears and worries down on papers so that the thought is transferred from the mind to the paper.
Usually writing down a thought would make the individual suffering from GAD tearful and fearful, as they are facing their worst fears in this process. However, this is to be expected and is healing.

Try the following steps to maintain a worry script:
- Write down your worst fear, the thoughts which are running around in your mind and which acts as an anxiety trigger. For instance, write down the fear of having a bad relationship with your mother, or about your loved one being in a car accident.
- Make the script as vivid and detailed as possible, using all your senses to bring in the details as much as possible. For instance, if you are writing about your loved one being in an accident, write how you would feel receiving the news. The fear, how your body would feel, how you would react.
- Try to write down your fears and worries for at least a half hour each day. Ensure you are not distracted from this important task whilst you are involved deeply in your feelings. Request your family to not disturb you, and turn off the ringer on your phone.
- Make sure you write a new script each day, going further and further into detail each day.

It is important to know that writing about your worst fears would not make them come true. This is just a thought process you are writing out to make your mind clear, and to make you emotionally stable. The goal is to make yourself care less and less the more you write.

- Be active!: Everybody says this, and yet it has to be repeated here. It is easy to hide and try to keep yourself busy at home. It has been noted that persons suffering from GAD tend to shy away from social activities, even if they step out of their houses.

However, it is important to keep in touch with friends and family when hit by anxiety. Friends and family form the backbone of a support system that would help you conquer anxiety.

Exercise and fresh air are always good for the mind, but more so when you are faced with anxiety. It refreshes your mind and helps your body to renew itself.

The social company acts as a mental booster. It provides a distraction from anxiety and gives you a shoulder to cry on if the need were to arise. Cutting yourself off from people who care would be the worst mistake to do when faced with GAD.

Substances to avoid or go-to to avoid anxiety – It is important to know which substances can increase or decrease anxiety. Here is a list of foods you would do well to keep away from:

Caffeine – this is a stimulant and would add to adrenaline already running in your body causing worsening anxiety

Sugar – Sugar can cause energy levels to fluctuate, which is a bad thing as anxiety itself causes energy levels to fluctuate. By taking in too much of sugar, you would be adding to the chaos in your body

Smoking – Tobacco in cigarettes also acts as a stimulant, causing problems just as coffee does

Alcohol – This would give a temporary release from the anxiety, by bringing in a sense of calm for a short time. However, alcohol by itself is a depressant and would cause anxiety to peak, requiring higher doses for it to work each time.

At the same time, do try to include the following items in your diet:

Flex Seeds

Fennel Seeds

Almonds

Green Vegetables

Avocado

Diet is not the only factor in controlling anxiety. However, it does play an important role. By messing up what you put into your body, you would mess up with your body's chemistry.

If you know someone who is suffering from GAD, do read on to know how you can help them overcome it.

Chapter Six – Helping Persons with Anxiety

At one point in time or the other in our lives, we must have all met someone who is suffering from anxiety. It could be a distant relation, an office colleague, or even a college professor. The disorder seems unreal and distant until someone close to us gets it too.

It is when we witness first-hand the effects of an anxiety disorder and understand how troubling and difficult it becomes to control the anxiety, that it dawns upon us that there is something wrong that needs to be treated.

Unfortunately, mental disorders come with a tag of social stigma. The society, in general, shies away from talking about Anxiety Disorders and Depression. Persons who do have any mental illness fear being labelled 'whack jobs' or 'crazy', and in turn, hide their troubles and pain from the public.

This is also the reason why people often do not seek treatment actively. Accepting the fact that you need treatment would be accepting that you have a mental illness. When the aim is to act normal and behave as if you are not affected by Anxiety Disorders, seeking treatment becomes a distant topic.

Another problem that is faced is the general public not being aware of what mental illnesses are. Persons suffering from mental problems have been sent to 'Madhouses' since medieval times. These Madhouses were houses of torture, where patients were confined to straitjackets and given electric shocks to 'cure' them.

In time, people's minds were conditioned to believe that all mental illnesses pointed toward insanity and that sufferers had to be sent to the Madhouse for confinement for public safety. In turn, people suffering from any and all mental illness began to hide their sickness.

Mental Problems, unlike physical illnesses, cannot be seen, and what cannot be seen is hard to understand. A gaping wound, a raging fever or a broken arm are physical attributes of physical illnesses. These are symptoms which can be seen, felt and understood.

When you can see that a person is suffering, and you can see what it is that they are suffering from, you can understand that it needs to be fixed. Medical aid is provided, and once the physical symptoms are gone, the patient is said to be healed.

In mental illness, the symptoms cannot be seen. Trembling of hands, breathlessness, anxiety and panic attacks are not commonly understood symptoms. Feeling fear without a reason, inability to control anxiety and feeling under the weather for days on end are not seen as symptoms of illness. These are instead looked at as something the sufferer should control themselves.

Let us compare a physical illness with that of a mental disorder. A physical illness such as a broken leg, or a strained muscle can be seen and felt. The redness of the skin can be observed, the swelling around the bruise can be seen. A person who fractures a leg wouldn't be told to 'run it off'. A person suffering from a severe cold wouldn't be told to sneeze it away.

Because mental disorders are that much more personal and not communicated, it is not easily understood that they too may have a biological reason, such as a chemical imbalance, or cell death.

A mental illness such as depression is regarded as a case of the blues. The patient is told they have no reason to be unhappy. When an individual suffers anxiety attacks, they are asked to 'not to think about it'. It does not seem silly to the society at large that they can ask the patient to just wish away or will away a mental disorder when they wouldn't imagine the same of a person suffering a physical ailment.

Many patients suffering from mental illness have claimed that observers do not think that 'they look sick enough'. Thus, the illness is trivialised, pushing the persons suffering from it to feel inadequate with growing sense of guilt and shame.

Oftentimes, persons who are suffering from Disorders such as anxiety or panic, or have been diagnosed with depression, are able to function at a normal level. Their condition need not necessarily affect their daily life, such as the inability to go to work or take care of their families. This does not mean that they are not suffering, however, just that they are fighting through their illness to lead a normal life.

However, it is misconstrued by a general society that a normally functioning person, though diagnosed with mental disorders, is perfectly fine. If the individual is not hospitalised, or suicidal, they are expected to be fine in all aspects.

For a person not suffering from mental disorders, it is important to remember not to compartmentalise these illnesses to a certain age, gender or social groups. A highly successful person who has a good job and a happy family could be suffering from depression. A small child with loving parents and a good school life could be getting anxiety attacks. An old woman with many grandchildren, a loving husband and a stable retirement income could be prone to panic attacks.

Nobody can understand what trigger any demographic group can encounter which can lead them to suffer from mental illness. And due to societal pressures, persons that are suffering often do not tell anyone about it.

This has led to disorders not being detected until it reaches advanced stages, causing the person to get much, much worse before they get treated.

A problem that is often encountered in daily life is the undermining of the mental health issues. For instance, the terms 'depression' and 'OCD' are treated with very little reverence. It is common to announce in general after an unhappy event in your life that you are 'depressed'. It could be any unhappy event, such as getting bad grades, not getting an expected promotion, or simply, having a bad day.

This means that commonly, depression is referred to as an emotion which means 'unhappy and displeasing'. However, depression is not simply to feel unhappy or to be displeased with an event in your life. To call it 'feeling sad' is an understatement, and insulting to the many persons that do actually suffer depression.

Similarly, persons suffering from a little nervousness describe themselves as feeling 'panicked'. Persons who have an inclination toward getting things right – such as lining up their clothes by colour, or having a clean desk, describe themselves as having OCD. This completely undermines the fact that OCD is a much more serious issue, where individuals who suffer from it spend hours arranging clothes by colour 'to get them just right', bound by the ritual to avoid crippling anxiety.

The Media also has played a dirty hand in spreading misunderstandings about mental health illnesses. Because not much knowledge is available on these disorders, the fictionalised stories shown in movies and dramas are perceived to be true.

A person suffering from depression is always described as suicidal in movies. Schizophrenia patients are depicted as murderers. When constantly fed such extreme, irrational stories about mental health problems, the general society becomes less and less able to understand the actual issues and problems related to mental disorders.

The media either sensationalises mental illnesses or gives them a pass completely. There is no information on anxiety disorder or panic disorders in any media source. Thus, there is very little understanding on the part of the people on what these disorders are. If they do understand something from it, it would be very much misunderstood and misinformed.

On the other hand, real people suffering from mental ailments continue to suffer because they do not wish to bring on social stigma. They begin to hide their real emotions and attempt to hide their illness. They feel as if the world is crashing in around them, and are unable to seek help.

Patients feel immense guilt about putting their loved ones through pain and hurt for them, and about the high costs of treatment that they are undergoing. And when they do not find people who understand what they are going through, the patients feel isolated and lonely. They feel cut off from society, and no matter how much they wish they were 'normal', they are unable to join in and leave their illness behind without help.

If you know someone who is going through a mental health problem, you would not wish to make them feel this way. Here are some simple ways in which you can show your support and be there for your family or friends.

- Do not tell a patient who is having an anxiety attack that the anxiety they suffer is because they insist on thinking of it – The illness that the patient is suffering from is not something they have asked for. Imagine asking a person who has been involved in a car accident and has suffered a few broken bones the same thing. It is not something they asked to have for either. And to get better, they need help and treatment.
Telling a person who is depressed that they need to be positive, or asking a person with GAD that they need to stop being anxious is like asking a blind person to name colours. He wants to, but he cannot. Just as a person suffering from GAD wants to be relaxed and happy, but cannot.
When they know what is wrong with them, that they are stuck in a loop of anxiety and anxious thoughts, which they are not able to get out of, makes them feel even guiltier than they already are. They are trying, hard. But it is just not in their hands to do so.
Telling a loved one diagnosed with Depression, GAD or Panic Disorder to 'stop thinking about it' is like telling a person with a fractured leg to 'stop thinking about it'. It not only won't help but instead, be the reason why the disorder could worsen.

- Don't let them feel guilty: They don't tell you, but every moment you are worried about them, they are dying of guilt. Their disorder is causing them as much pain as the guilt is. When a person is diagnosed with GAD, they feel hurt and pain for themselves and the agony they suffer each day. They also feel pain and hurt for the pain their loved ones are going through for them.

When a patient's husband is disturbed because of his wife's illness when a parent is emotional that their child is going through such horrible pain when a friend feels helpless in trying to make them feel better. The patient feels this pain acutely and feels themselves the cause of their hurt.

This guilt worsens the already chronic symptoms of anxiety and depression. If your loved one has GAD, assure them that you are not hurt because of them. Tell them you want to be there for them. Do not let them feel guilt at your cost. Sometimes, reassuring your loved one once or twice would not be enough.

Be there for them as much as required, reassuring them multiple times a day if needed, to let them know that they are all that matter and that they need not feel guilty for suffering an illness they have no control over.

Do not demean: Just as a person suffering from GAD falls in a loop of anxious thoughts and anxiety attacks, you could fall into a pattern of telling them to do this or that. You feel that you are helping them, and it makes you feel better to be doing something by advising the patient. It might be something important, for instance, if you are worried that they are suicidal, telling them to 'not attempt suicide'. Or because you have read online and found that walks are good for them.

However, it is important to remember that the patient already knows this. The patient knows they should not attempt suicide. They wish to resume their old lives themselves. They do not want to be locked up at home, they want to go out for walks and be with their friends too. They are just not able to.

What you should tell them is that you are 'there for them'. That if they need to talk, or be with someone, 'you are there'. If they need to be alone, 'you understand without judging'. If you feel that the patients suicidal, get them help, but do not tell them to not attempt suicide.

Be a Listening Ear – When suffering from mental illness, sometimes the patient gets an urge to talk, and sometimes to be alone. However, many times we do the mistake of trying to advise or talk over their feelings.
If a patient opens up to you, the worst mistake you could do is to tell them that they are feeling the wrong thing or to stop thinking that way. The patient is not feeling the way they are on purpose. They are just not able to stop thinking so.
And the fear of being judged and not being understood would make the patient not ever open up again, not only to you but to anybody at all.
When a patient begins to talk to you, listen to them, and be there. If they begin to cry, offer them a shoulder to lean on, and a non-judgemental ear for their agony. It would make a world of difference to them.

Research Anxiety – As we have seen here, there are many types of Anxiety Disorders which exist. A person suffering from PTSD does not have the same symptoms as a person suffering from GAD. Each would have their own triggers. Each would require its own treatment type and therapy.
If you're loved one has been diagnosed with an Anxiety Disorder, do research the different types of anxieties, and understand which type of ailment they are suffering from. When you know what their symptoms are, and what therapies would suit them best, you will be able to support them better.

It is not easy to see someone you love suffer, especially if you do not know how you can help them. It is never easy to be there without being able to do something concrete. These simple steps, however, would go a long way in helping them resolve their anxieties, and to know that someone who cares is not too far away.

You would have noticed that in many of these suggestions, we have mentioned the symptoms and care for persons suffering from Depression. Depression is like a dark monstrous cloud, which hovers over an individual, sapping away positivity and energy out of them.

The reason Depression is important here is that GAD is very often diagnosed as a secondary disorder caused by severe Depression. For this reason, it is important to know and understand Depression just as we understand GAD. Let us read on to know more about Depression.

Chapter Seven – Depression & GAD

Depression is a medical condition that affects the individual to negatively approach their feelings, thoughts and emotions. The reason we are discussing Depression in a book for Anxiety is that their symptoms are sometimes closely related. GAD is also an offshoot of Depression. This means that severe Depression can bring on GAD in an individual.

A very common disorder which usually affects, and worsens the pre-existing condition of Depression is GAD. It is often interchangeable. Severe GAD may lead to a person getting Depression, and severe Depression shoots off GAD as a side branch disorder.

As with Anxiety Disorders, Depression is also not an emotion that the individual is purposely bringing upon themselves.

Nobody wants to be unhappy or think negatively. However, a depressed person is incapable of thinking positively, or of finding happiness at even happy occasions. Persons suffering from this condition have described feeling trapped at the bottom of a well, or in a deep hole. They talk about having tall dark walls around them and finding it impossible to think of even getting out.

To listen to accounts from persons who are depressed, the symptoms vary from person to person. It is not necessary that the symptoms faced by one individual will be faced by all. Whilst one person may have a sudden loss of appetite and has difficulty sleeping, another may find it difficult to stay awake.

It is this variation in the symptoms that make it difficult to immediately identify that a person is suffering from Depression.

It is a disorder which is more than just feeling sad, or off-mood. That would be a big understatement, and akin to describing a fractured leg as a scratch. It is a serious illness caused by a variety of factors, ranging from changes in brain chemistry to genetics.

Unlike GAD, there isn't a trigger which causes Depression. It may be brought about by long-term issues, or a sudden loss. For instance, Maya has been unhappy with the way things are going on between her and her husband. Her husband is loving and warm and kind, but he has a short temper and snaps when he gets irritated. His snapping makes Maya very unhappy, and despite having discussed with him her problem, her husband is not able to change himself.

This has affected Maya deeply, because she loves her husband, and wishes he would not snap at her. This thought has remained deep inside of her for a long time and has slowly caused her to sink into depression.

At the same time, Ahmed's mother died in a car accident last week. He was very close to her and has not been able to deal with the loss. He finds himself feeling lost without her, and is not able to be happy. Whenever he does feel happy, he feels guilty for feeling so when his mother has died.

Here are some factors which usually cause Depression:

Changes in Brain Chemistry – This can happen for a number of reasons, such as medication that the patient is taking for some other purpose. There have been accounts where migraine medication or steroid have led to an imbalance of chemistry of the body, affecting the mind and leading to Depression.

Changes in Hormone Levels – When hormone levels fluctuate, especially post-delivery, or during menopause, they affect the mind, and the pituitary gland. This causes an imbalance in the overall enzymes and hormones required for normal functioning, leading to Depression. This is also the reason why many new parents suffer from Post-partum Depression.

Difficult Life Circumstances – When faced with intense grief or stress, such as the losses faced by persons during the 2009 Lehman Brother's bankruptcy period, they recede into a shell, to avoid shock to the mind and body. However much of a safety harness the shell might be, it leads to eventual Depression-like symptoms, and then, Depression and GAD.

Medical Conditions – Medical illnesses such as multiple sclerosis, HIV/AIDS, paralysis and cancer can lead a person to lose hope in life and recovery. This often leads to Depression due to the intense hopelessness and anguish at the condition of their health. This not only makes it harder to treat the medical illness but also makes it more complicated due to the Depression medication.

Genetic Inclination – If there is a history of persons in your family tree who have been affected by mental health illnesses, there is a distinct possibility of you getting it too. It is not necessary that you will have Depression or GAD, but the chances of being affected by life circumstances leading to Depression significantly increase.

Understanding that Depression is not just a simple emotion or a mood change is important for treatment. When a patient fails to get help in time, the symptoms worsen and often lead to other disorders such as GAD and Panic Disorder affecting the individual.

Here are some common symptoms affecting persons diagnosed with Depression:

- Weight loss or gain
- Loss of appetite
- Trouble falling asleep, or increased sleep during the day
- Loss of interest in hobbies and other areas of interest
- Fatigue
- Hopelessness
- Restlessness, agitation and feeling as if you're moving in slow motion
- GAD
- Panic attacks

As we have discussed earlier, it is not necessary for a patient to have all of the symptoms of depression. Symptoms often vary. It also depends on the type of depression that a person is suffering from.

Bipolar Disorder –

Sue is suffering from major mood swings over which she has no control. She does not know when she will feel happy, and when without reason, her mood will go down. When she is down, however, she feels without hope for her condition, and sits alone in a corner, not wanting to do anything.

She typically has lost her appetite and finds no joy except when her mood swings go up when she feels delirious with happiness and excitement. This cycle of mood swings is exhausting her physically.

Also known as Manic Depression, this condition is defined by mood swings affecting the individual, giving them highs and lows. When affected by the low mood, the person feels suffer intense symptoms of Depression. Medication is usually offered for controlling mood swings.

Seasonal Affective Disorder –

During the snowy months of dull November and December, Annie feels very low. The days are shortened, and even the festive season of Christmas does not cheer her up. Every time the days begin to stay dark for longer and longer hours each day, Annie feels a trepidation that her depression is going to descend upon her.

She is typically able to hold her emotions in check, but a couple of years previously, when her house was snowed in for two days, her depression became severe and she developed anxiety because of it. She was advised to take anti-depressants that year to help her get through the remainder of the winter season.

SAD occurs during the dull seasons of the year, such as winter. This can be treated with anti-depressants if it worsens, but usually, the patient recovers once the dull season is over.

Psychotic Depression –

John suffers from intense depression. He feels lost, sad and fatigued all the time. In the darkest periods of his condition, he sees people coming to take him away and lock him up. He feels paranoid every time he feels the hallucination coming on, and sobs for hours because he feels hopeless about his situation.

He feels delusional, and wonders if he will be locked up in a mental asylum because he is not able to control his mind.

Patients would suffer psychotic symptoms such as hallucination, delusions and paranoia. A combination of antidepressants and antipsychotic drugs is given to the patient in such cases.

Postpartum Depression –

Mary recently had a baby. Her husband is feeling depressed and uncertain about the future ever since. The doctor has said that new fathers have a surge of oxytocin in their bodies which can lead to postpartum depression due to hormonal imbalance.
Mary feels worried because her husband cannot seem to smile anymore, despite having been a very cheerful person before, and she sees that he has lost interest in working in the garage, which was something he loved to do before.

Postpartum Depression is caused by hormonal imbalances post the birth of a new baby. It is treated with anti-depressants to help the patient feel better until the hormones sort themselves out in the body's chemistry.

Major Depression –

Paul feels lonely and isolated from the world. He cannot understand why he is not able to smile anymore. When he sees happy videos or people laughing, he tries to join in but ends up breaking into tears instead.
He has lost his appetite, finding that even if he forces himself to eat, he cannot swallow. He is also beginning to get affected by anxiety now and finds himself sometimes having anxiety attacks which make him want to tear out his soul and run away. A pall of hopelessness has set over him, and he is

wondering if it is worth living through the agony his life seems to be stuck in.

If a person suffers depression without external factors such as seasonal changes, mood swings or psychotic attacks, they are diagnosed with major depression.

When a person is suffering from Depression, they need help and support from all factions of their life. If they are encouraged to not talk about their condition, or told that there are people who have suffered Depression and 'gotten over it', the disorder worsens.

It is true that some people recover from their Depression without the use of medicines. For others, the severity of Depression might be more. It is also possible that the symptoms for both patients were different, and that one may have been affected by GAD or Panic Disorder along with Depression, whereas the other was not.

Symptoms of Depression vary hugely between two different people, and common observers need to make note of this before they comment on their friends or families. You may be trying to be supportive, but not communicating the right way, or not being able to understand what your loved one is going through, you may end up worsening their Depression.

The treatment for Depression varies depending on the severity of the condition in the patient. The overall treatment is a mixture of therapy, medication and lifestyle changes.

Lifestyle Change is important, because if there are factors which you know are causing you to feel depressed, such as being obese, or relationship issues, you need to get them resolved to keep your Depression at bay.

- Exercise regularly, as being active releases endorphins and serotonin in your brain. These are the feel-good chemicals, and help keep your mind fresh and energised without giving in to negative thoughts.

- Make sure you eat well, especially food with glucose. Glucose is the food for the brain. Remember, if the brain is starved, Depression symptoms will worsen.

- Sleep at least eight hours a day to ensure your mind gets sufficient rest. Sleep deprivation causes restlessness, irritability, fatigue and mood swings.

- Try to remain active even if it is hard. Isolation is very bad for Depression, as it needs to be fought with the support of loved ones and friends.

Ensure that your doctor also rules out any complications caused by Depression. If you have been taking any medicine in the past year, do inform your doctor so that he can prescribe the correct treatment for you.

If possible, do avoid taking unnecessary drugs. Medicines prescribed by the doctor for health conditions cannot be avoided. However, do try not to take drugs for headaches or head colds. Treat these with home remedies, rather than resorting to pills and tablets.

Even though anti-depressants help in restoring the individual's mood for a time-being, it is not the ultimate answer to Depression. This condition is not only caused by chemical imbalances. There are many factors which cause Depression. It is necessary to identify the underlying factors through therapy to be completely cured.

If you know someone who is suffering from depression, do try and apply the following steps so that you can help them, without causing the symptoms to worsen.

Do not criticise or judge – Your loved one does not have a choice in feeling depressed. This is not something that they have brought upon themselves. When you judge them for not being able to be positive, or you criticise them for feeling fatigued, the sufferer feels further down. This can isolate them further in their condition.

Do not give them tough love – Telling your spouse to 'snap out of it' if they want you to stay in the relationship is not the answer to cure them of their depression. Telling someone to snap out of depression is the same as telling someone to snap out of having a fever. It is as hurtful as pushing away as someone who is suffering from AIDS or cancer.

Don't undermine their feelings – Do not invalidate what they are going through as they suffer. This is not a bad habit or a mistake they are making, but a struggle against a mental disorder.

Do not give advice – The advice you would give is something they already know. They know they should get out more, and that they need to try to think positive. But if it were possible for them, wouldn't they have done it already?

Do not compare – Do not compare someone who does not have Depression or someone who had Depression with the person who is actually going through it right now. It does not help.

Learn about Depression – This will help you understand them better. Depression is not a standard disorder. Like a fever, which rises and falls, the symptoms of depression also rise and wane.

Be patient with the patient – The person who is suffering needs you there for them, and just knowing that someone cares and understands is a big help. Do not snap at them because they are taking their time to heal. What is important to know is that at every moment, they are making an effort.

In the end, Depression is as bad a mental disorder as GAD. Its symptoms are agonising, and your loved one needs you there for support. It can be overcome, and there is hope.

The Author's Take on Depression

This book is important to the author because last year, he was diagnosed with severe depression made worse by GAD. It came upon him suddenly. There was no sadness to cause the condition, no loss, no shock or anything at all, that could make him even the slightest bit unhappy.

In fact, he had reached a golden period in his life at that time. He had given up his job to chase his dreams to start a career in writing.

And then, after a few days, he found myself hit by anxiety attacks. Full-blown anxiety, as if he was awaiting an exam result, or on a roller-coaster ride! Without reason. Without meaning. Without control.

And the depression! He would break into sobs for no reason..! His family would go crazy with worry, holding his hand and fighting tears themselves, as they found themselves helpless in the face of a disease all of them has never faced before.

This is his story. Everyone he knows shuns all talk about the helplessness he faced in those days. Hardly anybody outside his immediate family and friend circle even knows he had depression and GAD.

But he did. And with the support of all his loved ones, he pulled through.

Depression is still a taboo word in today's world. It's a disease which is to be kept under wraps, not to be spoken of. Anyone even suspected to have depression is quickly diverted. Tell them it's something else. Just a phase. A reaction to a medicine. A shock or a grieving. They're told to snap out of it.

That the Gods have given them in bountiful and they can't even be grateful for it.

When the author first found out that his symptoms led to GAD and Depression, he even tried to talk himself out of it. He told himself 'my breathlessness was due to a chronic cough. That my lack of appetite and weight loss were to be celebrated and were caused by my swimming. That my anxiety was a side effect of the Folic Acid tablets I'd been taking for my hair losses.

But when everything else failed, and he was forced to tell his family that he was returning home after meeting a psychiatrist. The sheer love and support he received from his family are unexplainable. Probably, that reduced his suffering to an extent. He could run up and down the stairs to get rid of the uneasiness and restlessness. He could cry and be helpless, and his family would sit with him and hold his hand to give him company.

And yet, not everyone is as lucky. How many times do people find themselves isolated because they are afraid to even let it be known that they have GAD? How many times do the medicines not work? How many times do family and friends abandon the patient, ridding themselves of a 'problem' they do not know how to handle…

And even when people think they're trying to be supportive, so many times, they're just not. You cannot tell a person having depression to 'not think about it'. You can't tell them to stop crying because frankly, they have no reason to cry. And you absolutely should not force them to sit in one place, when the panic caused by GAD urges them to run.

Depression is like being in a deep well. It feels dark everywhere. Trapped, claustrophobic, overwhelmed by the simplest of everyday tasks. When the GAD hit, the author felt like taking off his shirt or tear off his skin..! Being in his own body would be too stifling! Mundane tasks like drinking water or eating his favourite snack would give him anxiety.

A person who has depression needs support. They need a listening ear. A quiet listening ear, not one which keeps interrupting to give suggestions. Because this is not something that can just go away just like that. This is something that feels better the more you talk about it. Something that gets relieved with a bout of sobbing. Something that needs medical attention, and a willingness to be there, to understand the patient during the whole recovery…

The author was on anti-depressants and anti-anxiety medication for over four months after that, and it took a lot of effort and lifestyle changes to be healed. And yet, the smallest of worries he feels today make him worried if the GAD is returning. It is like after hitting your leg against a door, you worry someone might step on it. Similarly, every time he feels the slightest bit of anxiety, even normal anxiety, makes him worry that he might have GAD again.

If you know someone whom you think might be having depression, the best thing you can do is to listen to them. To encourage them to seek help. Because when you are not able to help yourself, it is best to seek help outside. And depression…

It is hard to keep it inside…

They say that having survived depression, a person becomes stronger. They lie. The author is a survivor. But he is also scared that it may happen to him again. That it may happen to someone close to him. That the support and love he found the last time might be missing on the next phase.

But at least he lost and found his way back. He struggled and fought himself back to a normal life. And though it has not made him stronger, he has gained a huge experience. An experience he would expect none to have like him but an experience he would want to share with all with only one motive – to help someone around who is suffering from the same.

Copyright 2017 by Christopher Adams - All rights reserved.

All rights Reserved. No part of this publication or the information in it may be quoted from or reproduced in any form by means such as printing, scanning, photocopying or otherwise without prior written permission of the copyright holder.

Disclaimer and Terms of Use: Effort has been made to ensure that the information in this book is accurate and complete, however, the author and the publisher do not warrant the accuracy of the information, text and graphics contained within the book due to the rapidly changing nature of science, research, known and unknown facts and internet. The Author and the publisher do not hold any responsibility for errors, omissions or contrary interpretation of the subject matter herein. This book is presented solely for motivational and informational purposes only.

www.ingramcontent.com/pod-product-compliance
Lightning Source LLC
Chambersburg PA
CBHW060806260726
48660CB00002B/804